ISBN 0-87666-991-7 • KW-030

CONTENTS

Photos:
Cover photos and all other color photos: Mervin F. Roberts
Kerry V. Donnelly: 41
Harry V. Lacey: 27, 31 (bottom), 33, 45, 49, 57, 61, 89;
Mervin F. Roberts: 76
Horst Mueller: Frontis, 18, 63;
Louise Van Der Meid: 19, 31 (top left); 32, 48, 60;

Distributed in the U.S. by T.F.H. Publications, Inc., 211 West Sylvania Avenue, P.O. Box 427, Neptune, N.J. 07753; in England by T.F.H. (Gt. Britain) Ltd., 13 Nutley Lane, Reigate, Surrey; in Canada to the book store and library trade by Beaverbooks, 953 Dillingham Road, Pickering, Ontario L1W 1Z7; in Canada to the pet trade by Rolf C. Hagen Ltd., 3225 Sartelon Street, Montreal 382, Quebec; in Southeast Asia by Y.W. Ong, 9 Lorong 36 Geylang, Singapore 14; in Australia and the South Pacific by Pet Imports Pty. Ltd., P.O. Box 149, Brookvale 2100, N.S.W., Australia; in South Africa by Valiant Publishers (Pty.) Ltd., P.O. Box 78236, Sandton City, 2146, South Africa; Published by T.F.H. Publications, Inc., Ltd., The British Crown Colony of Hong Kong.

Breeding
Society Finches

by Mervin F. Roberts

After two days of nest building, the first society egg was laid. (1) There was no preformed pad; the male simply carried grass stems to the basket and "wove" them into the wicker and into the ½ inch galvanized wire screen. The female is on her nest (2) but not incubating, just sitting. There are some bits of facial tissue and fresh greens but no feathers in the nest, although plenty of feathers were available. Nest construction continues while eggs are laid—one per day.

1

2

The male (3) stands over the nest where two incubated eggs have hatched and two are about to hatch. A one-day-old chick is already begging for food. Note that the eggs (4) are not in the same places they occupied in the previous picture. Probably the chicks moved them. The parents have been brooding the eggs and chicks constantly. These two chicks are now nearly three days old.

4

3

Preface

Poets and novelists may be able, willing and even anxious to accomplish their work with no outside interference or advice or help, but that is not the case here.

Over thirty selected magazine articles and twenty specialized books were reviewed and compared and read and frequently re-read. Breeders, importers and pet dealers were interviewed and a few dozen letters were written before this project took shape. I compared what I heard with what I read and with what was happening to my own birds in my own aviary. This is the product of all these experiences.

So many unsubstantiated ideas end up as dogma that separating the wheat from the chaff was not easy. Additionally, the state of the art is constantly changing, especially in genetics and systematic ornithology. I am sure you will discover gaps in our knowledge as you go through these pages. This then is a gauntlet you may be willing to pick up. Good luck!

I thank my ever-patient wife Edith, who this year begins her twenty-fifth year of reading and typing manuscripts for my pet-care books.

A.A. "Buzz" Paré of Miami and Daniel Kaye of Manchester, Connecticut were generous with their time and good thoughts. For all the help I got, I still claim full credit for the errors and omissions.

Mervin Roberts
Old Lyme, Connecticut 1979

A NOTE ABOUT THE PHOTOGRAPHS

This book was written and partly illustrated in an aviary created especially for photography of breeding birds. The enclosed area is eight feet by twelve feet and the ceiling slopes down from six feet to three feet. The floor is a continuous piece of nearly white kitchen-type textured material and two walls and the ceiling are plasterboard painted with white latex wall paint. The other two walls are ½-inch square galvanized wire mesh, and the outside flight is reached through the windows, which may be closed during cold weather. The outside flight is double-screened. The outside screen of the flight is a copper mesh mosquito netting, and on the inside of its 2x4" frame is again the ½-inch square galvanized wire mesh. The wooden floor of the flight is sloped to drain, ¼ inch per foot, and is covered with beach sand.

At the time the nesting photos were made, the aviary was occupied by six society finches, six zebra finches and four green singing finches. Eggs from Gouldian finches produced in an adjoining aviary were introduced into some nests.

The camera was a Nikon F2S and the lens most used was an f/3.5 55 mm "micro." Shutter speeds were 1/60 or 1/80 sec and diaphragm openings were f/22 or f/32. The film was Kodachrome ASA 64. No filters were used.

The light source filled the entire area with "strobe" flash of approximately 500 watt-seconds. Some light was "bounced" and some was direct. The calculated effective flash duration is perhaps 1/1500 second. The birds quickly adjusted to this blast of light and seemed, after a few flashes, to ignore it completely. The click of the solenoid on the shutter release made more of an impact than did the discharge of light.

Here a young chick is partly buried under its siblings, but this is not significant. Below, this same chick has nearly caught up with the others by its fifth day. Note that there are no droppings in the nest. The parents have removed (or eaten) this material. The blood vessel running over the crop is perfectly normal.

Introduction

Without any malicious intention to deflate your ego, I must say at the beginning that what you are about to accomplish has been accomplished so many times before and since so long ago that the beginnings are lost to memory and even lost to the written record. The society finch has been with us very long. The bird came from China and Japan around 1700. There were never any society finches in the wild. They would never be able to survive. The present day thinking is that the Bengalese evolved from the crossing of several species of the Lonchura family which gave fertile hybrids.

Hence some informed opinion has it that the society finch descends from crosses which included Philippine white-bellied, white-breasted, sharp-tailed and striated munias or mannikins. R.L. Restall in his *Finches and Other Seed Eating Birds* (Faber, London) tells us that the Bengalese is a domesticated striated munia which is also known as either the white-rumped mannikin or the sharp-tailed munia.

Since its ancestry is not completely agreed upon by all the authorities, its scientific name is also poorly established. In books going back only as far as 1963 you will find the society finch named:

Lonchura domestica (Bates and Busenbark, 1963)

Lonchura striata dom. (R.L. Restall, 1975)

Lonchura striata domestica (J. Buchan, 1975)

Lonchura striata acuticauda (J. Buchan, 1976)

Uroloncha domestica (V. Clear, 1966)

Munia domestica (K.J. Lawrence, circa 1973)

Lonchura means lance-like and refers to the shape of the long central tail feathers.

Striata means with alternate dark and light lines or with thread-like lines and refers to the pattern of the small feathers on parts of the head and chest. Actually "striated" is a better word for the zebra finch than it is for the society.

Domestica or dom. refers to the thoroughly domesticated aspect of this cagebird.

When we continue to look at the family tree the situation does not clear up at all. *Lonchura, Uroloncha* and *Munia* are all generic names which have been assigned at one recent time or another to the family Estrildidae or the family Ploceidae. Let's take a quick look at those families and another also closely related family.

In the class of birds (Aves) there are 27 orders and within those 27 orders there are about 8600 species. One of the 27 is the order called Passeriformes (the perching birds), and in it are 65 families. Three of these families concern us here.

Estrildidae (waxbills, mannikins) by recent count is represented by 107 species of small seed eaters, all of which are found in the Old World (Africa, Madagascar, Southeast Asia, East Indies, Australia).

Ploceidae (weaver finshes) includes weavers and whydahs, a total of about 130 species from Madagascar, Eurasia, Malaysia and introduced elsewhere, including North and South America.

The third closely related family is Fringillidae (grosbeaks, finches, buntings, sparrows) with about 375 species including the familiar and ever-popular canary.

You may be irritated as you read this because you haven't yet been told which family includes the genus *Lonchura*. The trouble is that the ornithologists who classify birds have changed the status of *Lonchura* and *Munia* several times and may well change them again as new information becomes available. In 1978 the weight of informed opinion favors Estrildidae over Fringillidae and Ploceidae.

The distinctions between these three closely related families are very technical and are of interest primarily to taxonomists (classifiers). Their names are here to help you with references to related birds in more scholarly texts. They are mentioned here also because within these closely related families you will find those species which will hybridize with societies and you will also find the species which are most likely to be successfully fostered or adopted by societies.

If you search in the old cage-bird literature you may find references to *Urolonchura*. This is an older generic name for some of the same birds. Other generic names of closely related forms which may crop up are *Spermestes, Euodice* and *Munia*. Most bird fanciers will use the words "society"and "Bengalese" interchangeably, and practically

Both parents (1) are on the nest and feeding the young. The male continues to add stems and leaves of dry grass. The nest is still clean. You will be looking at photographs of the same nest throughout this entire series of color pictures, but the background was covered with white paper to improve the light reflection for photography. The female (2) fed her "squeakers" and is about to take off. The air temperature was about 80°F. and so brooding was only on a now-and-then basis. The chicks are about six days old and their eyes are still closed.

2

1

The chicks are about a week old (3). Their eyes are not open. The pin feathers in the wings are showing some color. The nest is still clean. Note the whole husked yellow millet showing through the transparent skin of one the chicks.

The open mouth of a begging chick (4) is edged with white. The crop is full, and the eyes are not yet open. This is all normal.

3

4

everyone agrees that they are grouped somehow with mannikins and that munias are much the same. Bengal, you may remember is that part of India which faces the Bay of Bengal.

The dictionary does not help us much with mannikin when we look at our bird. We are simply told that mannikin is a variant spelling for manikin which means dwarf, puny or little man. Just to muddy the waters a little, it might be noted here that there is another group of birds called manakins or manikins (with a single rather than a double "n") and these are in no way related. The terms mannikin and munia are usually interchangeable and refer to birds of the genus *Lonchura*. All the recent *English* literature use the spelling mannikin.

It may be that the final word on this ancestry question was written way back in 1957. That was the year that E. Eisner wrote an article entitled "The Bengalese Finch" in *Aviculture Magazine*, volume 63, pages 101-108. According to Eisner's evidence our society finch is a cultivated form of a subspecies of the well-known striated finch, *Lonchura striata*. We are, according to Dr. Matthew M. Vriends, clearly dealing with mutations that happened by chance and then were developed by the Japanese. (Therefore, in quite a few languages these birds are referred to as Japanese finches—munies—mannikins, etc.) All crossings, as proven by Dr. Vriends, between society finches and *striata* are fertile.

Mannikins generally have short thick beaks and relatively modest coloration. Various species and genera are found in Australia, Africa, India, Ceylon, Burma and the Philippine Archipelago. Their thick bills suggest that they eat mainly seeds, but there is no finch that lives entirely on seed. As a matter of fact, they consume an enormous amount of insects, especially during the breeding season. They also rear their young almost entirely on insects. Hence some green food, some fruit and egg-food is taken, but the basic item of diet is seeds. In the wild all *Lonchura* species live mainly on ripe grass seeds. The whole breeding success depends on the ripening of the grass and the availability of insects.

Nowhere in this book will you find a strictly scientific description of the general features of this Bengalese or society finch or instructions about how to groom its nails or even how to treat its general diseases. This book is intended to help you breed these birds if you already have had some bird-keeping experience and now you wish to get more involved in the fine details of breeding this particular species.

A companion book entitled *Society Finches* covers those aspects of this bird not directly related to propagating it. There you will find answers to your questions about chlorine in water and how to keep birds from flying into windows.

The society finch is a good bird for a beginning breeder because it is hardy and prolific. It will breed in an aviary with room temperature or a large cage. It is also popular with advanced breeders for two reasons.

First it is variable in color and plumage. Its colors range from creamy white to dark chocolate with all sorts of white markings showing up. In fact no two marked society finches match each other, feather for feather. Also, societies are available with crests, sometimes called rosettes, on their heads. Both the feather structuring and the pigmentation follow Mendelian laws of genetics, and there is always the challenge to apply these laws to produce a new variety.

Second, true to its name, it is an extremely social bird, and with your careful control it may be used as a foster parent for other finches which lay eggs but then tend to desert their eggs or young. This is something similar to what a farmer accomplishes with "broody" hens when he wants chicks from the "laying" breeds.

The society finch is a good breeder and an ideal foster parent for many of the rarer finches that are not steady enough to be called *reliable* parents! As seen below, a small collection of finches can easily and happily be housed in a standard flight cage; the cage should be at least double the size of a standard canary cage.

Getting Started

A Bengalese hen in an old shoebox may lay an egg or two, but that is a far cry from our objective here. This book was written and illustrated to help you produce society finches of high quality generation after generation in sufficient numbers so that you can, if you wish, concentrate on colors or crests or production of foster parents for other, more difficult species.

Now let's go over the items under your control one at a time and make sure that you haven't overlooked anything that may rob you of your success. We will also consider the birds' instinctive behavior, which is something you cannot control but which you must learn to live with.

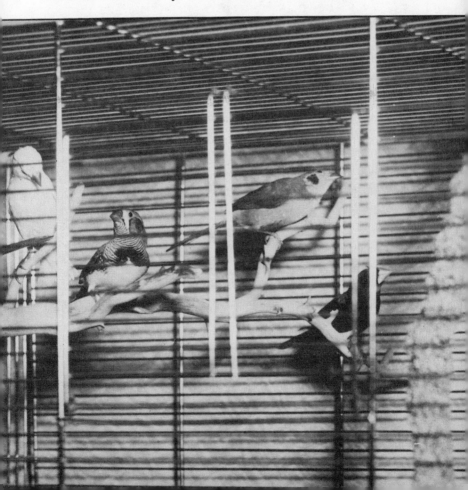

CHOOSING BREEDING STOCK

Pick a color. Match them or mix them—this is your choice except that you should be aware of the precautionary warning concerning blindness if you mate whites to produce whites. (White x white gives blind birds, not white x any other color).

Pick crested or non-crested but be aware that some authorities say the best cresteds come from one parent crested and one parent non-crested. Crested birds should not have bald spots. Crests should be uniformly feathered. Some crests are called double-crested. This is not easy to evaluate.

Pay for a known breeding pair or pay less and guess. Don't assume that two birds together on a perch are a pair. They may be very intimate boyfriends or girlfriends. The distinct difference between the sexes can only be noticed behaviorally by the dance of the male during the breeding season. Two males or two females can act as a pair, but in such cases no dancing or singing (by the male) will occur.

Pick fully feathered, vigorous, bright eyed, sleek, healthy looking, healthy acting birds. If you choose six at random the statistical possibility for at least one of the opposite sex is about 97%. Choose seven and the odds improve to 98.5% that there will be one pair, and of course a very good chance that there will in fact be several pairs.

The age of the birds is very important. They have to be healthy and fully feathered. Experienced breeders striving for highest quality show stock birds generally consider eight months to be the age to begin breeding society finches, to prevent egg binding.

When you choose a bird or a pair for yourself or when a judge evaluates birds in a show there are several things to watch for. Generally speaking, you too should want what the judge is looking for.

General good health. Clean feet without lumps or large scales. Nails of properly useful length, not corkscrewed.

Unbroken feathers, and of course full plumage. Bright, large, wide-open eyes. Erect carriage.

Society finch colors are easy to understand but less easy to recognize and still less easy to establish on the bird. You will find a description of the colors in the genetics glossary, but the pictures will probably be more helpful.

The standards of the British organization, the National Bengalese Fanciers Association, are also a great help not only for judging birds but also for choosing them when you make your purchases. You can obtain a copy of these standards by joining the Association; write to their secretary. At the time of this writing he is E.J. Hounslow, Esq., 2 Bridge Street, Griffithstown, Gwent, South Wales, Great Britain. The 1978 standards are also reprinted in the T.F.H. companion to this book entitled *Society Finches*.

A few basic aspects of currently available Bengalese colors you should keep in mind are:

There is no solid jet black, but according to Dr. Matthew M. Vriends, almost pure black can be established by crossing the Bengalese with bronze-winged mannikins. Very dark chocolate brown is easy to establish.

A tricolor—chocolate—fawn—white—is not with us except on rare occasions. There are however many bi-colors, chocolates, etc. in Germany, Holland, Belgium, Denmark and England.

A matched show pair is frequently made up of nest-mates and although they show well they are not the best source for brood stock.

A pied bird whose left side is a mirror image of the right (not front to back) is a potential prizewinner. A matched pair of mirror image pieds is an ideal which would certainly win prizes.

PICKING PAIRS

"Sexual dimorphism" is the term which refers to the obvious differences between the sexes. With birds this is generally a matter of plumage. Color or feather length is what varies, but not always.

On one hand we have peafowl where the peacock outshines the peahen. Birds-of-paradise, warblers and the pheasant are all examples of birds that display sexual dimorphism.

On the other hand, look at the herring gull, the bald eagle, the crow, the pigeon and the society finch. Here both sexes look alike. At least with the gull and the eagle the juveniles can be distinguished, but with the society finch they all look pretty much the same from the first full suit of feathers until their dying day.

Society finches seem to depend on performance to separate the boys from the girls. They dance a little, sort of stretchy and bouncy. They sing a little. Their song is not much; it's sort of squeaky, but it is more than what a female does. When two adult birds sing at each other, both are males. When neither sings, the chances are good that both are females.

Most society finches are compatible, and two of opposite sex are or soon will be a pair, especially if they are segregated from other society finches. Given the freedom of an aviary, three males and three females will work out to three pairs. In most cases there is not much *you* will need to do.

When a mature male and female society finch are confined together, and apart from others, the chances are excellent they will mate and breed and raise a clutch of young and continue to raise successive clutches of young. If after one clutch these two birds are introduced to a flock or if other birds are placed in the same enclosure with that first pair, the chances are very good that these two birds will remain paired. [Dr. Matthew M. Vriends' study in *De Vogelgids* (August 1975) shows that Bengalese mate for life.] Paired at least to the extent that no other male will inseminate that hen bird. One and/or the other of a pair might feed a fledgling which is not their own, but that's just their social behavior and is not the same as promiscuity, adultery, polyandry, polygyny or bigamy.

If you should separate such a pair and confine each with a stranger, apart and away from their former mates, it is probable that new pair bonds would be established in a few months. As with the previous bonds, they would last until broken by an "outside" force.

AGE FOR BREEDING

There are basically two distinct schools of thought about the age at which society finches should be bred. One school holds that the birds should be the ones to decide when they are "ready" to breed and that they will do so when they are sexually mature. Temperature, length of daylight hours and diet of course all have a profound effect, and it is entirely possible that under this system fledglings only a few months out of their own shells will breed and raise families. It is exactly for this reason that many experienced breeders of society finches make sure that the birds are not provided with nesting materials, nest boxes, etc., until the birds are between eight and twelve months old; they feel that letting the birds breed before that age is a mistake.

CAGE COMPANIONS

Societies are not pugnacious or nasty in any sense of the word. They are not apt to push, peck or otherwise harass any other small cage bird. They can hold their own in same-size company as well, so your choices for other birds in the aviary or roomy cage are not severely limited. For example, green singing finches, Gouldians and zebras in with societies will not adversely affect any of them, so keep them mixed if you simply need storage space for maturing juveniles or for holding young birds. Remember, though, that this business of bunching up juveniles or odd birds is not to be confused with your efforts directed toward breeding societies. Ideally, the best breeding situation calls for isolation of breeding pairs.

A cage companion you don't want is a mouse. Young mice can get through ½-inch square mesh. Once inside an aviary they will grow to a size where they cannot leave through the opening they used to enter.

Birds are also bothered by other cage companions you should eliminate. These are the many species of jointed-leg creatures. Here we consider the animals in the phylum Arthropoda including the class Insecta and the class Arachnida. The insects include mosquitoes, flies and lice. The arachnids include mites, ticks and spiders.

In both classes there are some scavengers and some parasites. "Some" is the wrong word—there are hundreds of species, some known, some unknown, some large enough to swat, others so small you need a microscope to merely see them and a high-power microscope to examine them. Don't bother, it will get you nowhere.

Bird lice are a bother which you will control, but many species of mites and all ticks are genuine enemies which you must actively fight. Fortunately, the life style of the parasitic mite helps you win the battle against him. It is a nocturnal feeder. During the night the mite sucks blood and during the day it hides and deposits eggs in crevices and cracks and nest boxes.

So, during the daylight hours your birds are rid of mites and you should take advantage of this fact to get rid of them. Place a white cotton rag over a cage of birds in the evening before you retire. Examine it the following morning after your breakfast. Mites will have crawled off the birds and settled in the folds of the cloth. Good. Fold up the cloth and burn it. In the morning you should put your mite-infested birds into a cage you recently sterilized with washing soda and boiling water and then sterilize the cage they had been in. Get into all the hiding places in the aviary with gamma benzene hexachloride. Do this once every ten days for three or four cycles, and you will have wiped out most or all the mites. Then do it once every other month or sooner if the mites show up again.

Ticks need to be picked off by hand or with tweezers; they can also be controlled by chemicals. Lice, mosquitoes and flies will succumb to pyrethrum compounds, paradichlorbenzene or a "no-pest" strip used intermittently. Remember that a light spray or dusting of pyrethrum is safe for all birds including society finches, but too much exposure to a no-pest strip or to gamma benzene hexachloride might possibly be dangerous for some of the more delicate species of birds. If convenient, move the birds out while any high-powered insecticide is working.

Paradichlorobenzene, the famous clothes moth control, is effective against lice and mites. Put some crystals near a louse-infested cage for a few days now and then, and if the treatment proves effective, continue it.

Some bird keepers report that they control pests with a spray they make up. It contains one part of Listerine and four parts of witch hazel, but there is not now and probably never will be one certain cut-and-dried sure control for these pests and parasites.

A standard canary cage is suitable for a few pairs of finches. The larger the cage the better! A long-lasting chrome, stainless steel or electroplated finish is much more satisfactory than a painted finish! Shown below is a double breeding cage with all the fittings and accessories used in breeding.

Cages

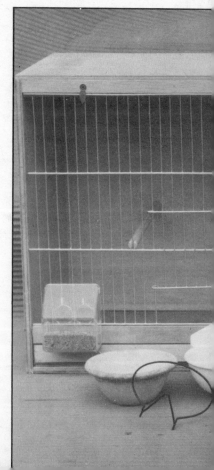

The practical minimum size cage for one pair of breeding societies is 15 by 15 by 24 inches long (about three cubic feet), and in it you should provide food, drinking water, grit, perches, a nest box or basket and a bathing dish continuously or at least daily for an hour.

Cages this approximate size are available through your pet dealer, if he does not already stock them. It doesn't matter if the cage is made of basket-type fibers, wood dowels or wire; regardless, an easily removable bottom tray is desirable for cage cleaning.

The cage you would use for one or two singing canaries or pet budgies is simply too small for breeding societies.

Another approach to caging breeders is to put as many as five or six pairs in a cage which measures 2 x 2 x 4 feet. Hang nest baskets in the upper corners and mid-height corners as well. Try to have one more nest site than you have pairs in the cage.

Still another approach is the walk-in aviary with nests hung from the walls and suspended from the ceiling. This is the arrangement which was chosen for making many of the illustrations used in this book simply because it made the photography easier. Of course a large flight is great for the birds. The exercise they get is surely a plus toward their general good health. Your maintenance efforts are also reduced since thirty or even a hundred birds will all eat from one tray, drink from one or two dishes and bathe in one bathtub. The drawbacks are that diseases will be transmitted faster and breeding birds will find territories harder to establish. This could lead to deserted nests and nests so full of eggs that no one bird could incubate them.

Regardless of the size of cage or aviary, some perches should be covered with sandpaper or other abrasives. Ideally the diameter of various perches should range from a lead pencil to that of your index finger so that the birds will not always flex their toes exactly the same way.

If you place potted plants in your large cage or aviary the birds will certainly spend a lot of time perching, picking and climbing. You should aim at something tough and not poisonous. A fruit tree, a privet, a forsythia or a honeysuckle bush might be good to try. Don't spend a lot of money on the tree and don't waste your effort on something which is in flower—you may discover that your societies prefer to have the leaves and petals on the floor, and they will surely accomplish their version of interior decoration in spite of your best laid plans.

By comparison with zebra finches, you may find that societies are somewhat better off in cages and zebras do somewhat better in aviaries—with respect to production.

Do not paint or varnish or otherwise treat aviary or nest-box wood with any aromatic substance. The natural wood smell is the least likely to offend the birds. In this respect, old aged lumber is more desirable than new material.

If you have an unheated aviary with an exposed flight and you live in an area where frosts are rare, your birds might just make it through the winter with roosting boxes located in protected places. Roosting boxes are similar to the nest boxes but twice as deep and with a small opening located below the center of the box and several perches, each long enough for two or three birds, inside. Remember there is that word "society" in their name.

When you hang nest boxes or baskets in an aviary or a large flight cage, you might consider hanging them at different heights. However, the birds will sometimes decide that the highest is best and instead of producing, they will use all their energy fighting for that one high nestbox, so more boxes in high places are required. If you don't have this problem, don't suggest it to your birds—they may never think of it.

One advantage of the cage over the aviary is that you will be able to observe and manage more closely your birds in a three cubic foot cage than in a small room-sized 600 cubic foot aviary. In case of disease you will probably notice it sooner. You will be able to capture the bird more readily and with less risk. You will be able to isolate sick specimens and sterilize a sick bird's quarters. You will be able to raise the temperature without having to heat "all outdoors."

When breeding commences, you again gain from close observation. You will have more opportunity to rescue babies in trouble, swap eggs or young to balance the load, to discover and remove infertile males, and find and perhaps help those hens that lay thin-shelled eggs.

The advantages of the aviary over the cage are that aviaries cost less per bird to build. You will have less work filling just one feeding dish, one grit dish, one bath and one waterer. The birds seem to enjoy the extended area for flight, but it doesn't necessarily make society finches produce more or better young.

If you remain active in the breeding of society finches through several generations of birds, it is almost certain that you will have at least a few cages even if you started with an aviary. The first will be an isolation cage for newly introduced birds, then perhaps a hospital cage with extra warmth and later one or two for breeders which you wish to keep apart because they are specially colored or crested.

Some species of birds have never been successfully propagated in cages, but this is not true of society finches, canaries or zebra finches. It is the opinion of many breeders of society finches that they do at least as well (and perhaps better) in cages than in walk-in aviaries.

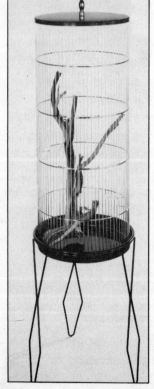

1

There is no real value in having a cage of complicated design (1) merely because it looks more attractive to the eye. Wire cages that are simple in line (2) have a good deal to recommend them when that is the type of cage that is felt desirable. Usually they are rather on the small side, although many different sizes can be made to order. The box-type cages (3) and (4) should NOT be used in a situation in which the temperature can fall to a level below freezing, because metal is a first-class conductor of both heat and cold.

2

3

4

31

A large flight cage for finches. This cage is ideal for four pairs. Like society finches, the cordon bleus shown below live almost entirely on small millet and spray millet and don't show much interest in other seeds. The cordon bleu (*Granatina bengalus*) has been cross-bred with the society finch.

Food

The basic finch diet is simple, but because it is simple doesn't mean it can be neglected. No finch can live on seed and lettuce alone—however he may enjoy these things. However, the basic diet of your finch is millet. There are several varieties and sizes of millet in the marketplace and you may find that the best source of grain is your pet shop where you can obtain one-pound cartons of a "finch mixture." This consists of millet, canary, rape, niger, oats and perhaps other grains as well. If you have more than thirty birds, you should be getting your millet in bulk—perhaps 25 pounds or even 50 at a time.

Which millet should you feed society finches? Try a few and settle for the one or two they favor. The nutrient values of all millets are about the same. The sizes and colors vary. Most of the color in millet is in the husk and your bird will remove the millet husk before it eats the grain anyway. Don't take color too seriously.

Buy clean grain—not damp, not water stained, not moldy. It may have some webs in it, and if you watch patiently, you may see movement. Not quite as much as the movement of Mexican jumping beans, but movement nevertheless. The webs and the movement mean that there are little white or creamy colored larvae in your birdseed. These larvae are perhaps as large around as a pencil-lead and to about five-eighths of an inch long. They have a cylindrical body with two rows of legs—much like a tiny inch worm, only they creep rather than inch about in the grain. Don't worry about a few of them, the birds will probably eat them along with the seeds. Later the larvae will pupate in cocoons and small moths will emerge to continue the cycle of life. I said "probably" because it is possible that your society finches may not eat those web "worms" in the grain.

If they do not eat the web "worms," then try recently molted soft mealworms.

If your birds will eat peanut butter, butter or margarine, this is great, a source of edible oil. Offer it to them spread on a piece of bread or toast or pound cake.

You should test your grain to assure that it is alive. Plant some as you would grass seed or put some on a wet towel for a few days to be sure that at least 75% of it germinates, that is, sprouts. Your birds will enjoy eating sprouted grain as a valuable diet supplement.

In addition to the millet in loose grain form, you may wish to give your birds the treat of millet on the stalk. This is called spray millet, and it is a plant species closely related to the millet seed you provide from the box or the bag, but the birds may gain something from the job of picking the grains out of the spray. They will certainly go at it avidly.

Don't forget cuttlebone, even though some birds will ignore it for months. Cuttlebone is a good source of calcium and also provides a natural grindstone for ever-growing beaks. Grits are taken from time to time to accumulate in the gizzard where they act to grind the food, but since society finches husk much or all of what they consume, the grit is not eaten in any large amounts. Silica sand is what you need, and it is often available mixed with charcoal, oystershells and various minerals. Much of the grits go out with droppings but what the bird does take is vital to its life processes.

You may wish to buy some insurance in the form of liquid vitamin additives. Some successful breeders swear by vitamins, others consider them not too important. Probably an unsupplemented diet of millet needs a vitamin and mineral boost, but a broad-based menu including treats such as hard-boiled eggs, fresh greens such as kale, spinach, green lettuce, carrot tops, grass cuttings, fruit, whole wheat bread, oatmeal, rape seed, niger, poppy seed and wild bird mixtures from time to time will obviate the need for vitamin supplements.

The protein content of millet is a trifle lower than what breeding and baby society finches ideally should have. One additional problem is that the protein in millet lacks certain amino acids. This is why experienced breeders will offer a variety of oily seeds including rape, niger, poppy and sesame to supplement the basic millet diet. In case you wondered why oil seeds are recommended to increase protein in the diet, it is a fact that most high fat-content seeds are also high in protein. Canary seed is also a desirable supplement even though it is not high in oil.

Interestingly, canary seed (*Phalaris canariensis*) happens to be high in those amino acids which are low in millet (*Panicum miliaceum*). I might mention here also that spray millet is in fact not a *Panicum* but is classified in another genus of plants and is scientifically called *Setaria italica*. Hard-boiled egg is also a valuable diet supplement for millet-fed breeders and nestlings because of its high protein content.

The following information has been adopted from data found in Winton, A.L. and K.B., *The Structure and Composition of Foods* 1939, New York, John Wiley and Sons and Petrak, Margaret L., *Diseases of Cage and Aviary Birds* 1969, Philadelphia, Lea and Febiger.

Grain, including Husk	Protein	Fat	Fiber	Ash	Carbohydrate, other than fiber
Rice	8%	2	9	5	65
Millet	13	2	9	4	62
Canary Seed	14	4	21	10	27
Spray Millet	15	6	11	6	51
Sunflower	15	28	29	3	17
Fennel	16	12	14	9	32
Niger	19	43	14	3	12
Rape	20	45	6	4	18
Caraway	20	17	16	7	29
Poppy	21	50	5	7	10
Sesame	21	47	5	6	19
Hemp	22	30	19	5	16
Gold of Pleasure	22	31	11	7	22
Flax	24	37	6	4	22

These values will vary with the minerals and fertilizers in the soil, growth rate and rainfall, but even so they do serve to explain why experienced breeders will offer more than just millet to their birds.

It has been suggested that the ratio of protein for breeding finches should be about 19% of the diet. Actually when the bird shucks the husk from millet, its fiber content will go down several percentage points and protein will increase.

Living seed undergoes chemical changes when it germinates and in this state it becomes a beneficial supplement to the basic dry millet. This is especially valuable when feeding birds which are, in turn, feeding nestlings.

For each bird involved, soak one-half teaspoon of the same seed you are presently feeding in room temperature tap water for 24 hours and then spread it out on a damp towel for an additional 24 hours. Now call this product "half-germinated" seed and feed it to your birds and especially to nestlings.

Let the same grain remain on the damp towel for several additional days and call it "sprouted" seed, also excellent as a diet supplement for your birds. Let them eat as much of it as they wish after you acclimate them to it over the course of a week or so of offering only small quantities.

This advice about small quantities when introducing a "new" food is good advice for any supplement or treat or diet change for any captive bird. Most important, if you plan to add or subtract an item from the diet of your birds, do it long before they begin to breed. They should be thoroughly accustomed to the food they are getting before they begin to feed their babies. For example, you may have neglected to provide grit until the eggs hatch. Well, that's too bad, but what might be even worse would happen if you suddenly introduced the grit at that time and the adults in blissful ignorance pumped a fatal dose of grit into a newly hatched chick.

A precaution is a caution you should consider in advance of an emergency or a catastrophe. So do that.

One aspect of nutrition, well known but frequently overlooked by beginners in aviculture is that calcium in bones and egg shells requires vitamin D in order to be properly utilized. That is the reason that milk, a high calcium food, is often "fortified" with vitamin D. This vitamin D then is the anti-rachitic or preventative for rickets, the disease of soft bones.

This natural chemical substance, vitamin D, is often called the sunlight vitamin because it is so closely tied in with solar rays. In fact, the process for making the vitamin D in milk hinges on irradiation (exposure) by certain wave lengths of ultra-violet light naturally emitted by the sun or artificially created by special electrical discharge lamps.

Now these words could have been written in any one of three chapters of this book. We will consider it here in *Food,* but we could have justifiably located it in *Light* or in *Cages*. The point is simply that direct unfiltered sunlight seems to help birds to produce their own vitamin D. So, you should if possible give your birds the advantage of a screened aviary, part of which is exposed to direct sunlight at least a few hours daily. A more sophisticated technique would be to provide ultra-violet light from a lamp—this is difficult, expensive and could be dangerous if overdone. The third method is to provide foods and food supplements which are known to be rich in the various complex factions of this important substance. You may, if you wish, supplement their diet by adding irradiated cod liver oil to some of the grain you feed, or you might use a vitamin D concentrate available from your pet dealer or pharmacist. As you can see, there are several routes to follow; choose the one that is most convenient and don't neglect it.

As an aside of considerable interest to people who avoid eating foods containing cholesterol, it should be pointed out that as long ago as 1924, studies of cholesterol and vitamin D showed that ". . .cholesterol, which accompanies most animal fats, and the analogous constituents of vegetable oils, became active antirachitically when they were exposed to ultra-violet radiation." This quotation is from the fourteenth edition of the *Encyclopaedia Britannica*. Actually it is not the cholesterol itself that is activated but a minor component associated with it and known as ergosterol.

Don't worry about cholesterol in your birds' diet causing heart disease. It is very likely that by the time you read this book there will be ample evidence to prove that the quantity of cholesterol that plugs the circulatory system of your pet bird or yourself has nothing to do with the quantity of cholesterol in the diet. Animals can and do manufacture cholesterol regardless of what they eat.

The other vitamins necessary for the health and fertility of your birds (A, B, C and E) will come naturally if you show intelligent care in providing fresh raw green vegetables, a variety of living seeds (test them occasionally to be sure they sprout) and diet supplements such as fruit, hard-boiled or scrambled eggs and wheat germ.

WATER

The few diseases and parasites your birds may have or may get are often transmitted from one bird to another when fecal matter gets into the food or drinking water. This is something you must (and easily can) control. Don't arrange the cage or aviary so that a perch is located over another perch or over food or water. Do change water dishes frequently and wash them thoroughly before you refill them.

Provide bathing water at room temperature separate from drinking water and remove the bath tub promptly after it has been used. One half inch or so is ample depth for the bathing water.

Don't expect baby society finches to bathe until they are fully fledged—three months would be about the youngest age at which they might voluntarily go into water, and a month more or less will not make any difference to the health of your bird.

If you have been giving your birds water from a dish deeper than ½ inch, take it away when fledglings appear.

The first time you try to
catch and band a fledgling
you will surely wonder if
you dare, but bear in mind
that over the centuries
many people, far clumsier,
have managed with pa-
tience and gentle firmness.
You will also.

*Catching
and
Banding*

First, to avoid any possible misunderstanding, do not trap or even possess any wild finches in the U.S.A. It is against federal law to own or traffic in native wild birds. A Philadelphia lawyer might find a few loopholes, but a Philadelphia judge might find the lawyer was wrong. So, just don't catch or own native birds, and keep out of jail—this is on the statute books as a felony!

If your pet escapes you should write it off—the chances of recovery don't justify chasing it down.

If your problem is simply inside your aviary or large cage, the first approach should be at night. With patience you may be able to pick up the bird you want in your hand.

If you must net a bird, buy a net from a dealer who specializes in them. The fabric should be closely woven to avoid entanglements—a ¼-inch mesh would be coarse for finches. The size and shape of the hoop depends on your aviary. One foot square or one foot in diameter is about as small as most people can effectively use. The larger the hoop, the easier the catch, but as the hoop gets larger it gets unwieldy and perches get in the way.

The hoop should be wrapped with a soft fabric so that if your bird collides with or is caught under the hoop, it will not suffer broken bones.

Ideally, you should make your captures at night by hand.

BANDING

If you are serious about breeding more than one pair of society finches you should keep track of your birds with bands. There are two basic types of bands. The first type of band is the permanent or "closed" band which is a seamless ring—usually of aluminum and anodized in many permanent colors which you can obtain custom made with your initials and some system of numbering embossed into the metal. The ring band remains on the bird for its lifetime. You will slip it on a fledgling when it is between four and seven days old and certainly before it is twelve days old by sliding it over the three forward toes and then past the pad of the foot and up the shank of the lower leg until it clears the rear toenail. You may need a broomstraw to help get the ring past that rear toe. The ring then slips down on the lower leg and remains loose but permanently attached for the life of the bird. Breeders will order bands in a different color every year so that the age will be apparent even without close examination. Of course, the number of the band should be recorded in a ledger along with others of that clutch and the numbers of the parent birds.

The second type of band has some sort of seam somewhere. It is a plastic springy coil which usually bears a number or a letter. Of course these too are available in various colors. Seam bands or "open" bands are usually used by breeders just to keep track of pairs or sexes—combinations of colors on left or right or both feet will provide the information at a glance. Of course, they may be removed at the end of a breeding season.

Another type of coil band made of plastic is simply a colored spring coil which bears no number. This too is useful in an aviary where many pairs might otherwise not be sortable. Still another version of the "seam" band is used by banders of wild birds and it is a numbered metal band which is closed loosely around the adult bird's shank with a pliers-type tool. You pay your money and you take your choice. Pet shops that specialize in small birds can get these bands for you or lead you to a source of them. So can the advertisements in aviculture magazines and members of the bird breeders' club which you might want to join.

The first time you try to band a fledgling you will surely wonder if you dare, but bear in mind that over the centuries many people, far clumsier, managed with patience and gentle firmness. You will also.

One suggestion: sit down at a desk or table to do the job, at least for the first time. If you are off your feet, your hands will be steadier. If you can brace your arms or elbows on a smooth level surface you will be steadier still. Second suggestion: don't permit anyne who hasn't already banded one to be in the same room with you the first time you band a baby bird. It really is not that difficult and with these suggestions it will be still easier.

When your permanently banded bird wins a prize, any doubts about the justification for banding will vanish, absolutely.

Firefinches and weavers are trusting little birds that soon lose any initial nervousness if care is taken not to scare them by sudden movements and if they are allowed time to gain confidence according to their own inclination. Red-headed finches from South Africa (below) have frequently become available. Females lack the red on the head and the well-defined spots on the chest.

Varieties of Society Finches

In nature there is genetic variation. Sometimes it is as subtle as fingerprints or ear shapes. Sometimes it is as conspicuous as albinism. When organisms are not protected in captivity, the less fit are less prone to survive, less prone to reproduce themselves.

Now look at the society finch. Its ancestors were possibly members of several subspecies, so there is a large "pool" of latent genetic material which can easily be brought out by thoughtful selective breeding. In case you have not thought of it just this way, consider that thoughtful selective breeding is just another name for the application of Mendelian principles.

Also, the society finch matures rapidly, is hardy, prolific and long-lived. With all these things going for it (genetically speaking), there should be small wonder that many of them do not resemble any species of wild bird. You may have to add a few words to your avicultural vocabulary. The colored and white specimens are called pied. A self-colored bird has various shades of the same colored feathers all over its body. Cream, tan, fawn, cinnamon, chocolate and light mocha are good descriptive words for the most common self colors. Then there are dilutes which are pale versions, blending in white, and also there is pure white.

In addition to the variation among society finches, there is variation resulting from crosses between society and other finches. Since we don't know precisely what a society finch is—in terms of its ancestry—it would be awkward to say "hybrid" when we refer to the product of a mating of a society with, say a Philippine white-breasted mannikin, a sharp tailed mannikin or perhaps its most probable progenitor, a wild striated mannikin.

In addition to the color variability of societies, crested birds are also available. The feathers on the head are arranged as rosettes and some breeders have even produced birds with rosette crests on the sides of the throat and neck. Of course, pigeon and canary and poultry fanciers have been doing this sort of thing for centuries. There is hardly a limit to what can be accomplished if you have the intelligence and patience—a little luck also helps.

One awkwardness about variation in society finches is that there is no variation to distinguish the sexes. Males, females (and immature birds once they are fully fledged) look pretty much alike. If you hold an adult female bird and feel the spacing of the pelvic girdle, you may be able to note a wider space between those bones (to permit passage of eggs). This is difficult and of doubtful value. The best way to determine sex is by observing behavior. Males dance and sing. When they mate, the male makes the advances and

46

does most of the nest building. Don't look for a *rigid* schedule for incubating eggs as with the pigeon. Societies simply take turns on the eggs; when one is off the other is on and sometimes both are on. True, males do tend to favor night-time setting, but you should not count on it.

Variety of color and plumage is subject to some limitations mentioned earlier. If you wish to produce white society finches you should go at it with the knowledge that whites are believed by some breeders to be vulnerable to eye cataracts and may go blind by the age of two or three years. White crossed with white results in blind birds that will not survive long.

Another item for you to be aware of along this line is that some experienced breeders say that crested birds should be produced from one crested parent and one non-crested parent. If both parent birds are crested, they say that the offspring have a tendency to be partly bald. At least one successful breeder of crested societies says that this is not so and that it is perfectly appropriate to mate cresteds. This is something you will have to resolve for yourself. Many people breed societies without regard to colors and simply enjoy the surprise of seeing what hatches.

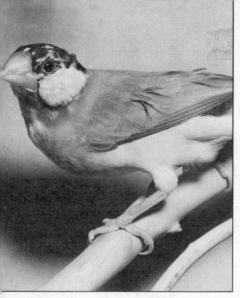

Rice birds are among the hardiest and most popular of the larger finches. Zebra finches (below) are among the most productive of all breeding birds in captivity. The male is very attractive with the bright cheek patch, chestnut flanks with white spots, and zebra lines on the chest. The female lacks these features and usually does not have even the indistinct dark markings on the chest.

Inheritance

The inheritance of traits or characteristics from parents to offspring can be summed up as follows. The characteristics of a living individual are controlled by submicroscopic chemical units (genes) present in the chromosomes of all the cells. Chromosomes and the genes contained in them occur in the body as chromosome or gene pairs (one member coming from the male and the other from the female parent). By means of a very complicated cell division during reproduction, the chromosome pairs (gene pairs too) are separated from each other and received by the egg or by the sperm. When fertilization occurs (egg and sperm combine) the embryo will then have chromosome pairs and gene pairs once more.

Each species of organism has a specific number of chromosomes in their cells. For example, budgies and lovebirds have 58 pairs of chromosomes, some finches 28 pairs, and the domesticated chicken 76 pairs! One cannot imagine the number of genes present in the chromosomes and the possible combination of genes resulting in the development of characters in an individual.

By comparison with variation found in the chicken or the pigeon or the budgerigar or even the canary, our society finch has not come very far. Its colors are either chocolate or cinnamon-fawn with either color shading to white or splashed with white. There are no blues, greens, yellows, reds, or solid jet blacks. Its feather arrangement doesn't give us fantails or feathered feet. There are no long necks or compressed bodies, no variation in bill shape. The most variation we can count on in society finches is the aforementioned.

Even this color range is strictly limited. There are "selfs" (various shades of one tint of color) and there are mottled birds, but the mottling (pied) is limited to white and again just one tint of brown. When you begin to search for a tri-color of cinnamon, chocolate and white—don't hold your breath—*you* are likely to turn blue sooner. The pictures of societies and closely related species should help you to anticipate what you normally can expect from a clutch of eggs.

If we get careless with language, unnecessary confusion or arguments frequently result. This chapter is mainly concerned with color and two words well known to painters and fashion conscious ladies. These are shade and hue. Shade is a matter of comparative darkness. For example, the sky is often a very pale shade of cobalt blue. An old-fashioned medicine bottle is often a very dark shade of the same tint of cobalt blue.

Hue is a matter of comparing or combining two parts of the spectrum of colors. Brown can be combined with orange. Call that hue of color cinnamon. Brown can be combined with green. Call that hue olive-brown or hazel.

All right, look at the pictures as you remind yourself that:

Dilute is a pale *shade* of either chocolate or fawn.

Fawn is a pale cinnamon-orange *hue* of chocolate.

Dilute is a light shade of a color and in society finches it shades all the way to white.

The best evidence right now suggests that the hue of brown color we call chocolate is dominant over all other colors. If one gene for chocolate is present, the bird will be chocolate regardless of whether other color genes, which may be present, are dilute or fawn or white.

There is much we don't know about society finch color. For example, all the experts tell us that chocolate is dominant, but breeders have all sorts of troubles producing a 100% domesticated society finch which is 100% free of white flecks, especially near the bill. This trait is usually eliminated in solid color birds (selfs) by crossing the society finch with the wild striated mannikin. The fertile offspring tend to be free of white flecks.

All-over white (selfs) is recessive to both fawn and chocolate, but to stop here would leave the story before it really ended.

There are really at least two whites. You may have a white derived from chocolate. It will have dark brown eyes. Or you may have a white derived from fawns. It will have ruby eyes. These two whites came by their whiteness down different chromosomal roads and a product of their mating is not necessarily white, even though both parents are genetically pure white. You will just have to accept this statement at its face value. The explanation is to be found in highly technical textbooks.

Dilute chocolate is recessive to normal chocolate and dominant over fawn, but it has not been proven to be sex-linked in the same way that available information presently leads us to believe dilute fawn is sex-linked. This sounds like a Philadelphia lawyer talking, but in the case of society finches, all the facts are not yet sorted; in fact, they are not even known.

There are no established strains of tri-color society finches but once in a while one does turn up and of course its owner will try to propagate tri-colors from it. So far, they have not been successful. Another challenge.

If you wish to go much further you will have to read other books about genetics and selective breeding. You *must* learn the language; it really is not that difficult. There are several conventions and abbreviations used to simplify and shorten the description of the genetic make-up of a bird. Look at the glossary. It is arranged alphabetically and includes the terms you will need to get started and quite a few of the other less common terms you may also encounter.

Let us ignore the possibility of a dramatic mutation and proceed to predict the color outcome of a mating of two society finches. We will use a relatively simple procedure with a few easy examples and then if you wish you can go on alone from there.

It should be remembered as we proceed that we are looking here at statistical probabilities and there is no positive assurance that every nestful of mixed colors will be in the predicted ratio. What we are sure of is that over the long run the odds will prove true.

If this gets the least bit sticky for you, stop and read the glossary of genetic terms and then come back and complete this chapter. Your other option is to stop reading right now and raise a few nests of birds. Record the colors of the parents and the offspring. Then read this chapter.

Let "C" be the gene for the normal dominant chocolate color and "c" be the gene for the recessive fawn color. A chocolate bird might be represented by CC if it is pure (homozygous) chocolate. It might also be chocolate color but have a recessive gene c for the fawn color trait. This is something you cannot see, but it is represented as Cc and we call that individual "heterozygous."

A fawn bird is represented by the genetic abbreviation "cc." It is homozygous for the recessive "c" which is the symbol for fawn color.

Let us mate two chocolate society finches. Each bird is either homozygous (pure) or heterozygous (split) for color. Assume for this first example that both are pure. The designation for each bird is CC.

Draw up a little chart thus:

The male_____CC

The female_____CC

	C	C
C	CC	CC
C	CC	CC

The expected ratio of offspring resulting from the mating of two chocolate societies not carrying any color recessives is 100% chocolate.

Next, as we wander down the garden path together, let's see what happens if both birds are heterozygous (split) for fawn.

Of the four possibles we get:

	C	c
C	CC	Cc
c	Cc	cc

One CC = 25%
Two Cc = 50%
One cc = 25%

This cross will, over the long haul, produce:
    25% fawn birds "cc"
    25% chocolate homozygous "CC" pure
    50% chocolate heterozygous "Cc" split,
    the same as their parents were.

Now, let's consider a cross between one pure homozygous recessive fawn cc and one split heterozygous chocolate Cc.

	C	c
c	Cc	cc
c	Cc	cc

The offspring will appear in the ratio of two split heterozygous chocolates and two fawns.

Now you have stuck your toe in the water and it feels fine, but Mother Nature made things much more interesting and difficult by hooking some of the color genes onto sex chromosomes.

The best informed opinion at the moment has it that dilute fawn is a sex-linked recessive characteristic. This means, in birds, that dilute fawn is a genetic characteristic carried on the male "x" chromosome. Now, a male bird is a male because it has two such "x" chromosomes in each involved cell. A female bird is a female because in her cells there is one "x" and associated "y" chromosome.

Let's take a brief look at the interactions and their results. First we need some symbols and some definitions.

Sex-linked recessive color trait—Dilute fawn = d

Normal fawn color = D

Male sex chromosome = x

Female sex chromosome = y

A male then is charted thus: xx

A female is charted thus: xy

A male with this dilute character on one chromosome is x^dx^D and the trait is hidden from your view because it is recessive. For it to be apparent on the bird, both x chromosomes would need the superscript "d" and x^dx^d. A male with no dilute in its genetic makeup would be shown as x^Dx^D. Since a female has but one x chromosome and this color trait is tied to the x, it needs but one "d" to show its true colors. That is, x^dy is a female with dilute fawn color.

For sex-linked crosses, the procedure is a trifle more complicated than in the previous example. Start with a pure normal fawn male. Always write the symbols for the male first. Since dilute fawn which interests us is presently believed to be sex-linked we carry the color on a sex chromosome.

x is one sex chromosome. The male has two, xx.
Superscript D is the dominant sex linked color and
Superscript d is the recessive dilute sex linked color.
y is the other sex chromosome. The female has one y and one x, so we designate her xy.
A male xx is a pure normal fawn, so he is designated $x^D x^D$.
A female xy is also a pure normal fawn, so she is designated $x^D y$. There is no sex linked color gene carried on the y chromosome.
We now mate a male xx with a female xy. That is, xx and xy.

Reading across—female
Reading down-male

We expect a ratio of 50% males and 50% females when we mate a pair of society finches. Simple.

	x	y
x	xx	xy
x	xx	xy

And now the sex linked color trait for dilute fawn. Mate a normal fawn male $x^D x^D$ with a dilute fawn female $x^d y$. d = dilute, D = fawn.

Reading across—female
Reading down—male

Statistically, two females will be fawn, x^Dy. Two males will be fawn with a recessive heterozygous dilute hidden in their genetic pool, x^Dx^d.

	x^d	y
x^D	x^Dx^d	x^Dy
x^D	x^Dx^d	x^Dy

This time we will switch just one little submicroscopic gene and see what happens. Start with two fawn birds. The male is fawn, heterozygous for dilute and the female is normal fawn.

Reading across—female
Reading down—male

One female x^dy is fawn dilute. One female x^Dy is fawn normal. Both males are fawn but one x^dx^D is heterozygous and the other is homozygous.

	x^D	y
x^d	x^dx^D	x^dy
x^D	x^Dx^D	x^Dy

GLOSSARY FOR
COLOR GENETICS
OF SOCIETY FINCHES

Albino—There are presently no albino (pink-eyed white) society finches. Note that brown-eyed or ruby-eyed whites are not albinos.

Back-cross—The mating of an individual to one of its parents. Frequently used with hybrids (splits) to establish a new strain or breed.

Dilute—A weak color which blends or shades into white. There is no such thing as self chocolate dilute because dilute includes white and so it cannot be called self.

Dominant—The genetic characteristic which is apparent (phenotype) even if it is derived from only one of the two genes which determine that particular trait.

F_1, F_2—First and second generations.

Fawn—Also called cinnamon. This is not a diluted chocolate but is more like the light reddish brown of cinnamon. Fawn is recessive to chocolate.

Genotype—The complete genetic make-up of an animal, not necessarily just what shows. See "split."

Heterozygous—One gene differs from its companion for a particular trait. The dominant gene determines what the organism looks like. The recessive gene is hidden or latent.

Homozygous—Both genes for a particular trait are alike. This makes an individual "pure" for that trait regardless of whether it is dominant or recessive.

Inbreeding—The mating of relatives to establish a pure breed.

Mutation—A sudden genetic change which happens in an egg or sperm cell. A mutant is an individual exhibiting the "new" trait or characteristic.

Normal—Also a layman's term and one not used consistently by all authors. It generally means dominant homozygous, but some authors use it when they simply mean dominant.

Pied—Color mixed with white. Pied colors are pied chocolate, pied fawn, dilute pied chocolate and dilute pied fawn.

Phenotype—What an individual looks like irrespective of its genetic constitution.

Recessive—A genetic trait which is not apparent in an individual unless both of a pair of genes are the same.

Self—Solid color. The self colors are chocolate, fawn, and self white.

Sex-linked Recessive—A recessive trait whose gene is carried on the same chromosome which also controls sex.

Split—A layman's term for heterozygous. It usually appears in print with a diagonal slash. Chocolate/dilute would be referred to as chocolate split for dilute.

Variation—The differences within a species. For example—crests, chocolate, fawn, pied, dilute.

White—Absence of color but not albino. White may have brown eyes or ruby eyes. Self white is recessive to all other colors, but if we mate a brown-eyed white with a ruby-eyed white we may not obtain any white offspring.

Society finches have been cross-bred with a number of different finch species, one of which is the African silverbill, *Euodice malabarica cantans.* No cross-breedings between society finches and a member of the genus *Estrilda* (black-cheeked waxbill, *Estrilda erythronotus*, is shown below) have been reported, however.

Hybrids

One traditional definition of a species is that it is a population of similar individuals that produce fertile and similar offspring. This particular definition falls apart (or the genus *Lonchura* needs revision) when we consider the society finch. Fertile offspring have been reported from crosses of societies and other members of the genus *Lonchura*. Additionally, societies mated with several other similar looking species produce infertile young. This latter situation is akin to the mating of a mare and a jack (a female horse and a male ass) producing a mule. Now, a "mule" means sterile or infertile. Some canary-finch crosses are deliberately made because the "mule" that results is such a

wonderful singer. Here then, for what it is worth, is a list gleaned from several sources, of species which when mated with society finches produce living young. In some cases the offspring are fertile and in others they are not but the available information on fertility is not always clear and unequivocal.

White-rumped mannikin or Sharp-tailed finch—*Lonchura striata acuticauda*

Common spice finch—*Lonchura punctulata* (Cocks of this species mated to society hens have been successful)

Black-beaked bronze mannikin—*Lonchura leucogastroides* (Fertile offspring)

Chestnut-breasted finch—*Lonchura castaneothorax*

Black-headed mannikin—*Lonchura malacca atricapilla*

Bronze-winged mannikin—*Spermestes cucullatus*

Rufous-backed mannikin—*Spermestes bicolor nigriceps* (This species has been reported to have crossed "with other species of mannikins")

Long-tailed Grassfinch—*Poephilia acuticauda*

Parson finch—*Poephila cincta*

Bicheno finch—*Stizoptera bichenovi*

Zebra finch—*Taeniopygia guttata*

Cherry finch—*Aidemosyne modesta*

Diamond sparrow—*Stagonopleura guttata*

Star Finch—*Bathilda ruficauda*

African Silverbill—*Euodice malabarica cantans*

Bib Finch—*Lemuresthes nana*

Cordon Bleu—*Granatina bengalus*

Bicheno finch, *Stizoptera bichenovi;* this species has been cross-bred with the society finch.

Propinquity

This is a great word for aviculturists, unfortunately not used or applied as frequently as it might be. In case you have forgotten, Webster's dictionary defines it as the "state of being near . . . nearness of nature, disposition, interests, etc; affinity; as, *propinquity* as an aid to courtship."

Propinquity as an aid to courtship is the whole point here. If you want to help establish a strong pair bond, then keep that pair together and apart from others on a remote desert island or, lacking a desert island, keep them in close and private quarters. Remember that this is not a book about California condors who might fly a hundred miles in search of a meal or a mate. Here the bird's whole universe, food, grits, water, perch, room to stretch, nesting materials and nest site can all be contained in a package encompassing only three cubic feet.

If you wish to produce a strain of tri-color crested society finches, you would be infinitely better off with sixty cubic feet consisting of 20 cages each of three cubic feet than you would if you created an aviary six feet high, eight feet wide and twelve feet long. That aviary would occupy 576 cubic feet and you would be no better off if you put the same number—20 pairs of birds—into it. A wall six feet high and ten feet long with one foot wide shelves one foot apart would, in theory, suffice for such an arrangement.

In practice you would need an additional 20% of space to allow for clearance and wall thicknesses, but the point remains unassailable—if you are aiming to breed society finches and space is a factor, you should design the accommodations around cages rather than an open aviary.

If your society finches have nothing else to do, and no one to molest them, their success ratio in the nest will go up. Some aviculturists might argue in general terms that as productivity goes up, quality will go down, but you must bear in mind that this particular species of bird, like the canary, has been bred in cages for a long time, and it is practically as domesticated as a henhouse chicken.

It may be possible that two pairs of society finches kept together will produce more young per year than twice the output of either pair kept alone. This is true of the budgerigar, also a highly social species, and is worth your consideration if production is your aim. The above is mere speculation by the author with no supporting data. However, it is known that when 2 pairs are put in one breeding cage, the birds fight; this does not occur when 3 or more pairs are put together.

Companions for even such a relatively peaceful species as the society finch must be chosen with care, especially if the birds are going to be maintained in an aviary in which they are forced into proximity with one another.

Mixing Birds in Aviaries

If you set up your bird breeding establishment around an aviary rather than around a bird-room full of cages, you should bear in mind that you have a management responsibility which does not exist when one pair is kept in its own cage. The precise nature of this responsibility will evolve as you proceed and as your birds establish territories and pecking orders. Situations will change as hormones flow and songs are sung and nests are built and eggs are dropped.

This short chapter will not tell you many specific do's and don'ts because it is impossible to anticipate all the things that may happen. Here then, is a challenge in bird keeping. You and you alone must watch your birds and adjust their environment to suit their needs.

For example, your society finch aviary may have twenty adult birds in it. It is impossible to determine sex at a glance, but you assume that with twenty there is a 95% probability that there are at least eight pairs. The unpaired four birds are then all of the same sex. This could lead to pairing of extra females and incubation of infertile eggs or it could lead to pestering of the available mated females by extra unmated males, if that is how the statistical cookie crumbled for you.

Another example of a management problem caused by mixing is what happens when another species is introduced. Societies will breed all year round if you let them, but others may have a seasonal schedule which they follow closely. Peaceful companions in July may raise hell with each other in November. Don't assume that time stands still in the aviary. The gentle inoffensive juvenile green singing finches you added to your aviary in June will get along fine with the society finches—ignoring their nests completely and feeding side by side until, as they mature and begin to plan ahead, a shortage of nests or a shortage of desirable nesting locations could lead to trouble.

This short precautionary note is inserted simply to remind you that in nature, and especially in a breeding aviary, there is no *status quo*. So what can you do to anticipate the problems which may arise?

1.) Keep an empty cage available to segregate either the domineering breeders or the pesky interferers.

2.) Avoid overstocking; it is truly a temptation that faces all of us.

3.) Hang an over-abundance of nest boxes and baskets in the aviary to reduce competition for desirable sites.

Watch your birds, *thoughtfully*. Most of what first looks like meaningless flittering and twittering is in fact their fascinating and consistent and complicated lifestyle.

Bullies at the water or food dishes are a beginner's problem. Hopefully, you have solved that before you get into this breeding activity, but in point of fact most societies are perfectly social and eat, drink and make merry at the feeder, the water and even in the nest.

Nests

Your society finches will build nests. That is the only nearly dogmatic statement I can make about society finch nests, and as I write it I realize that the "weasel" word *nearly* automatically crept in.

Sometimes societies lay their eggs in nests built by others. Still, we can't call them nesting parasites. A nesting parasite is more in the style of the cowbird or some cuckoos where a whole lifestyle and even anatomical details of egg mimicry and short incubation time are coupled with cold blooded premeditated murder to accomplish the incubation of their eggs and the raising of their young.

Societies are simply terribly social. They don't establish strictly defined territories and then fight hard to maintain them. They remind me of the charm of "old style" hippies who acted like "what's mine is yours and what's yours is mine," but left unthought or perhaps unsaid, "but I don't have anything." Societies, like hippies, have much charm and neither of them strongly demonstrate much territoriality. Perhaps this is the first evolutionary step toward nest parasitism.

Well, right here and now, your long-domesticated strain of society finches is well named. They will incubate the eggs of their own making or others' and they will raise and wean the hatchlings, no matter whose they really were, all this in nests they didn't necessarily build themselves. You will have trouble recognizing pairs; one isolated pair of society finches in either an aviary or a cage will resemble each other so closely that behavior alone will be the only clue to their sex.

In either an aviary or in a breeding cage the need for a man-made container for nesting is about the same. Your society finch will be more prone to build in the container you furnish than in the fork of a tree or on a window sill or in the corner of the floor of the cage. You will also discover that societies would prefer to be as far from the floor as is possible. So that is where you should hang the container, and in addition to the various basket-like containers, you might well also try a homemade or store-bought wooden box. It should measure, inside, five by five by six inches high, and the upper half of the front should be open. A landing perch is not especially important—these birds are agile in flight and can pop right into the box. If the birds are crowded and seem to push each other, you might extend the sides and top in order to provide a little additional privacy. Two inches of overhang should suffice.

Nest material should be available for the male to perform his architectural work. Yes, the *male*. Please bear in mind as you read this book that it was written specifically to help you raise society finches and the behavior of these birds is unlike that of many other seed-eating aviary birds.

Horsehair is one excellent nest material. The short strands of nesting thread (which look like white cotton) available in your pet shop are also favored by society finches. Ideally there should be a variety of dry grass stems and soft thin substances for your birds to choose from.

If you provide only coarse grass stems there will be a problem, since although the birds will try to soften the stems, they will still end up with a nest cup whose bottom openings are larger than the eggs. Some eggs will thus be lost or jammed in the bottom of the nest and will not get the warmth needed for incubation. A slight rolling of eggs probably takes place in an ideal incubation situation. This is nature's way of preventing adhesions. Additionally, an egg incubated while standing on end is liable not to hatch. So, for all these reasons, the nest cup should end up with a relatively smooth bottom. Coarse hay just doesn't work for nest bottoms even though some societies will choose it for the sides of their nests.

The birds, if provided with proportionally more stiff material than they would like to have, will try to make the best of it—but why make things difficult? A pre-formed horsehair nest pad available from some pet dealers who specialize in small birds is a good investment.

Sun-dried garden-grass clippings are favored by some birds as nest-lining material. If you should hang an armful in a rack on the aviary wall for the birds to pick through, it is possible that one enterprising cock will entice his mate to lay right in it. If the same finely cut soft hay is placed on the aviary floor, you will not have the rack nests to contend with, but your establishment will tend to look messy to some people. Take your choice.

Another good liner for a society finch nest is a mat of the lint you will find in a clothes dryer. It is felt-like, soft, often mostly cotton and certainly sterile. Still another good nesting material is made from burlap potato and grain bags. Cut it into two-inch squares and then pull apart the strands. Really long pieces are a hazard since your bird may get tangled in them.

The nest may be in a cardboard box or in a hay rack or in a wooden "finch box" or in a gourd or a gourd-shaped basket or a coconut or even in a cup-shaped open basket. I have had a pair of societies select an open canary nest cup which was right next to a perfectly lovely, especially designed, covered-top, finch nesting basket. Subsequently, another pair of birds took over the "proper" finch basket.

The isolated pair will probably enjoy some preliminary billing and a few songs by the male—not much music to our ears, but it seems to satisfy the female. Soon they will copulate; usually she will be perched on a twig. Nest-site selection and nest-building will then commence in earnest. The nest will be partly built when, about five days after the act of mating, the first egg is deposited. Work on the nest will continue as eggs accumulate, perhaps to the count of four or even five.

A second nest may be constructed near the one with the eggs to house the bird which is not on the eggs at night. Sometimes it will appear that both birds are simultaneously incubating the eggs. Certainly they are sitting together on top of the clutch, but more about that in the chapter on incubation.

Societies may become impatient—another slight suggestion to me that after an additional 250 years of domestication they will lose their strong instinct to follow-through with the full cycle of raising a family. This impatience may be manifested in a covering-over with nesting material of the clutch being incubated and the laying of an entirely new clutch right on top of the old one. Zebra finches are also known to do this, especially in an aviary.

Just look at what selective breeding did for the Leghorn chicken. Today it is simply an egg laying machine. It lays infertile eggs (as many as 200 per year) and even if the hen was mated and the eggs were fertile it still would not get broody. This was accompanied by selective breeding which really got going only since the time of Christopher Columbus.

If you suspect that an abandonment of this type is about to take place and you wish to stop it, remove the female and hopefully with her gone—out of sight, out of hearing, out of mind—the male will carry on his family duties and raise the youngsters alone.

If a nest in an aviary appears especially crowded and many do, put an armful of hay on the floor under it to act as a cushion and perhaps you can rescue a nestling which was crowded out.

When you arrange nests in a large cage or aviary, don't be too certain that your choice is their choice. All advice might be that societies want covered nests and then you will find that your covered nests are completely ignored and the open canary cups are favored. Don't fight it.

If you cannot induce any birds to utilize a nest that looks

perfectly good to you, don't chuck it until you try putting a decoy in it. Buy a few dummy eggs from your pet dealer or bird supplier or use an infertile one left over from another clutch and put it in that nest cup. This might trigger a few ideas in the mind of the male finch in search of a nest site.

Try moving an unsuccessful nest to a new location, sometimes a matter of only a foot will make a difference. Up is better than down. Dim may be better than bright and small is frequently better than large.

The male society finch is a persistent nest builder, and although the female may give him a little help from time to time, it is he who you will readily identify as *the* builder. During the daylight hours the hen is most likely to be incubating eggs, and when he isn't spelling her for a lunch break, he is likely to be employed nest-building. Yes, that's right. He will continue to build the nest during the incubation period. And the stuff he carries there will strain your credulity. He will try to fly off with a stem of grass which is planted and growing in a pot. When he gets to the end of his tether, he will come crashing down, but a few minutes later he will be at it again. A soft green lettuce or spinach leaf will also take wing, even though it spans a greater distance than do his wings.

Don't bother to help the bird, it will only encourage him to try to lift still larger, still heavier materials for the nest. It may appear that he is trying to bury his mate and clutch of eggs.

The Eggs

Society finch eggs are white, slightly glossy and the minor diameter is not midway between the ends. Ornithologists call them conical. This can also be said of zebra and Gouldian eggs, but zebra eggs tend to be a trifle chalkier and shorter while Gouldian eggs are larger in both dimensions.

A few eggs sampled at random measured as follows:

	Society	Gouldian	Zebra
Major diameter	.585	.675	.560
in inches	.566	.647	.555
Minor diameter	.435	.475	.440
in inches	.424	.472	.441

The reason for this egg description, in view of the fact that it is beyond your control, is that if you have these three species together in an aviary or a large breeding cage, a nest might well contain eggs from all three. Although society and zebra eggs are incubated for about two weeks and Gouldians require several additional days, it is possible to raise all three in one nest. It is worth noting that these three species lay *white* eggs. Now, ornithologists tell us that white eggs generally come from birds that nest in dark places. For two classic examples, look at woodpeckers whose nests are invariably in the deep hollows of trees and they have white eggs, whereas the robin who builds an open cup on a tree limb lays a blue-colored egg.

This suggests that these birds naturally lay in covered nests. Another clue suggesting that the nest interiors are naturally dark is that newly hatched society finches have bright (perhaps phosphorescent) marks in their mouths which might facilitate the delivery of food in a darkened nest.

INCUBATION

The female lays the eggs and sits on them and in 13 days they hatch. Simple, but sad to say, this is far from true, especially for society finches. Let's try again with a little more detail.

While the nest is being built by the male and perhaps also by one or two male society finch on-lookers with a little help from the female, the female deposits one white egg. It may have a creamy pink cast to it; this might be shell color or more likely it is just the color of the yolk transmitted through the thin shell.

Even before that egg was deposited, one or both birds (and perhaps even the onlooker) had been sitting in the nest. That is to say, the eggless nest might have been occupied by one or sometimes (especially at night) two and perhaps even three adult birds. This is quite a tight situation for a small bird's nest, but those are "just the facts, Ma'am" as Sergeant Friday would say on that famous television program.

Eggs from one female are deposited at the rate of one every day or perhaps skipping a day now and again until about five eggs are laid. It is absolutely impossible to chart a rigid program—the birds simply don't rigidly conform. Many birds, including finches, have hotspots on their breasts which are warm enough to trigger egg development only if the adult bird pushes aside the insulating layer of feathers so that the warm skin actually touches the egg shell. The real incubation process begins on the day or the day after the last egg is laid and it extends for about thirteen or fourteen days. The female seems to put in more hours on the nest than the male. He works the night shift.

By the time those eggs hatch—say fifteen days after the last egg in the clutch was laid—you may discover that the male has built a second nest and that the female laid a second clutch in it and is incubating this second clutch day and night while the male remains with the first clutch as they hatch out. Probably the wisest thing for the aviculturist to do is—nothing. It is still possible that everything will work out. It is entirely possible that if you have several pairs of societies in one large cage or aviary you will never unravel the ancestry of the fledglings.

If just prior to hatching time your birds show a special interest in taking baths, it may be that they sense dry eggs and this is their way of correcting the problem. Good! Let them bathe to their heart's content.

The eggs will open up from the inside, that is to say, they need no help, just parental warmth and perhaps that extra moisture. Hatchling birds are naturally furnished with a tiny sharp "tooth" on the tip of the upper beak which cuts through the membrane and shell. The blind, naked embryo bird actually chips a ring around the shell, and it then pops up after the hatchling takes a deep breath. The adult birds remove the empty shell halves from the nest, and the next chapter logically is entitled "Bringing up Baby."

As an afterthought I might mention that you should expect an 80% success ratio from your eggs. Over the long haul, eight of every ten eggs of your pet society finches should hatch and fly out of the nest. If they don't, you should cage separate pairs and stop all that social interplay until you find the culprit or the other reasons for your lack of success.

If you find that your live eggs are not hatching and you have no clue as to the trouble, try misting the nest with a fine spray of water at a temeprature of about 95⁰ Fahrenheit. The water may aid the chick to chip through its shell and the temperature is suggested so that you don't chill it to death while you are helping it to live.

Society finch egg flanked on either side by one-day-old and three-day-old chicks.

Commence spraying or let's call it "misting," on the twelfth day of incubation and continue on a once-daily basis until you get a decent hatch or until all hope is gone.

If your birds bathe frequently *and* the humidity is high, this misting might not be necessary, but if all else fails, try it.

Bringing up Baby

Now, these next few paragraphs will possibly lead to controversial communications. It is a gray area. Much more needs to be known. Now that the disclaimer has been written, let's get on with it. To begin with, a bit of history—it should be stated that the thoughts here are not entirely original but were suggested in print at least as far back as 1969 when Mrs. Katherine Tottenham of Bideford Zoo, Devon, England wrote a piece for Margaret Petrak's book.

When a society finch hatches, it has a little food supply (yolk) remaining from what was inside the egg shell. The chick might not be fed for the first 24 hours of life. It survives on its remaining yolk-sac reserve. The first food it gets from its parents (with male and female cooperating in feeding the chicks) is smaller in particle size than single grains of millet. You can actually see the yellowish food in the crops of hatchlings. It is not in the form of granules but rather like a thick milky fluid with some tiny lumps. It has the consistency of a "thin" cooked cereal.

When you watch an adult society finch eat, you will notice that it picks up a grain of millet, holds it between upper and lower bill, manipulates it with the tongue and cracks off the husk which falls away in one or two pieces. The entire husked grain is then swallowed. It is not crushed or cracked before it is swallowed. This grain then is (with water) the source of food for the chick. It is swallowed and descends as far as the crop of the parent bird, where it is held for at least long enough for the parent to get from the feed dish to the nest. But if you watch closely you may discover that is not precisely what happens. The parent does not go directly from the grain dish to the nest. It eats, perhaps drinks and then suns itself or preens its feathers or

77

perches a while. The robin brings the worm directly, the osprey brings the fish directly, but the finch hesitates. That grain in the crop destined for the chick does not descend to the gizzard for grinding. If it ever got that far down the alimentary canal it could never get back up. Anatomically impossible. No, it remains in the crop. I use the word crop carelessly because we all know what a crop is. Actually in a finch it is a diverticulum with two lobes. Some authors call it a fusiform crop. You will see it as two yellow streaks beside and above the neck of a chick.

Now, let's look at some other birds for a moment. Pigeons, doves and parrots swallow grain, nuts and seeds and then they subsequently regurgitate a milky food which nourishes the chicks. The male penguin does something a trifle different, he produces a secretion which sustains his chick while his mate is off fishing. She may be gone a few days and he has no cache of food set aside to carry himself or his chick. He survives, and the chick thrives on "penguin milk."

Back now to finch chicks. Watch the parent feed the baby. The chicks squeak insistently while the parent stands in the nest and works its throat and bill. The motion suggests that the parent is regurgitating softened moistened grains (perhaps partially digested) and breaking them into smaller particles for feeding to the hatchlings. At this time soft food—cooked cereals, soft cakes, hard-boiled or scrambled egg pushed through a sieve and high protein insect food—would reduce the burden on the parents and might even reduce infant mortality. Here in the cage we are not looking for survival of the fittest (a selection process), but we are striving for maximum production of healthy birds under controlled conditions.

Without supporting evidence it is suggested here that the adult finch does partially digest grain with water, mucus and enzymes in its crop and that what it regurgitates for at least the first few days of the life of the hatchling is more like pigeon milk than simply husked and cracked millet grains.

When the adult bird looks down the throat of a nestling, it sees some luminous markings inside the mouth which are reputed to help in aiming the food, especially in darkened nests. Many authors of bird-care books imply that luminous markings are unique to the species described, but this is not true—all (or practically all) nestling sparrow-like (passerine) birds have these glowing areas—the color, shape, area and location might vary but not enough to inhibit a society finch adult from feeding a Gouldian foster baby.

When the eyes open, the nestling is about the right size to get its permanent metal band. If you go at it sooner, you will find that the band may slip off as easily as you slipped it on. If you hesitate too long you may have a problem passing it over the pad of the foot.

Your nestling society finch will become a fledgling in three or four weeks, depending on food supply, temperature, daylight hours or perhaps the phase of the moon. The parents will continue to feed it even as it leaves its nest. It may, as it learns to fly, spend its daylight hours at the feeder or water supply or on perches away from the nest and then return "home" at night.

By this time the adults may have another clutch of eggs in the same or another nest nearby—and on we go.

In some books you may find the statement that the baby society finches will be out of the nest in two or three weeks. This is possible but don't be upset if yours are retarded—so long as the babies have their crops filled several times a day, they will make it even if they remain in the nest a full four weeks.

Fledglings are (technically) the young birds, feathered and just ready to try their wings for the first time. The transitive verb *fledge* means to rear or care for a bird until its plumage is developed so that it can fly. *Fledgling* and *fledge* are often used loosely by aviculturists, but no great harm results.

Now let's use another word and take another look at a society finch: *nestling*. This is a young bird which has not yet abandoned its nest. Nestling is a word we can easily put a handle on since the bird ceases to be a nestling when it leaves its nest.

On the day it hatches your society finch nestling is probably very tired. It spent a good part of the previous day chipping its shell. This is the process of cutting through the membranes and the shell itself, using a tiny sharp point on the end of its upper beak to accomplish the job. Remember that this project is all done from the inside out and the cut is amazingly straight and uniform. Visualize yourself tightly squeezed in a barrel with the lid on and with a small saw attached to your head. Now get out of that barrel. Every bird has had this experience.

The society finch parents will not give it much help—there really isn't much they (or you) can do from the outside. Once the chick is out, or nearly out, the parents will remove the empty halves of the shell. These will be eaten (recycled is the popular term today) or at least carried away from the nest and discarded. You will not find empty society finch eggshells near the nest.

The other material which is removed is fecal matter. Since the young birds release it in a membrane sac it is not difficult for the parents to cart   off or eat it (recycle it). The nest will be absolutely clean, at least for their first week.

About a week after hatching you will begin to notice an accumulation of droppings from the birds around the perimeter of the cup. It seems that the babies soon learn not to foul the center of their own nest and they turn their tails toward the outer edge of the nest before they defecate.

The blind, naked nestlings may have little fluffy down patches showing on their bodies when they are three days old, but the first feathers that look like feathers will be evident on the seventh or eighth day. These will be the wing flight feathers—the primaries—and they appear before the eyelids open. It is possible that the nestlings are able to recognize their parents and also discriminate between day and night before their eyelids actually open, but sharp retinal images are not possible until then, at the earliest.

When the chicks are about twelve days old you may see them preen their primary flight feathers which are now beginning to burst out along the long bones of the wing. They will spend many of their waking hours squeaking for food even as they are being fed. You will witness feeding of babies not only by both parents, but by interested passers-by as well.

You should continue to supplement the diet of the adults with hard-boiled or scrambled egg pulverized through a sieve and/or a nestling food purchased from your pet shop. Some societies might eat soft mealworms recently shed, but whether they do or they don't is not especially important.

If you didn't put closed bands on your chicks when they were about a week old, you might ring your birds now with "open" aluminum bands or plastic spirals. They are certainly inexpensive and the convenience of knowing the pedigree of a bird is something you will not regret. You may remember your first chick but by the time you have twenty, you will be pairing nestmates if you aren't careful.

Three sleeping chicks (1). The ear openings may come as a surprise to someone who has never before examined unfeathered chicks. The chocolate bird (2) is a parent. The fawn and white is a visitor. Note that as the pin feathers in the wings erupt the nest suddenly begins to get dirty. The eyes of the chicks are about to open.

1

2

The chicks' eyes (3) are opening, and the tail feathers are erupting. One chick hasn't quite caught up with the others in development. In this case it never will. Two chicks (4) are squeaking for food, and one is silent because it is getting a charge of regurgitated millet from the female parent.

3

4

Foster Parents

Once you master the breeding of society finches and you feel you want other species and more challenge, *don't get rid of your breeders.* One good way to produce some of the more difficult finches in your home is to use society finches as foster parents.

Keep several nesting pairs for every laying female Gouldian (or whatever) and when the eggs begin to accumulate, substitute them for the society eggs. These birds will tolerate a good deal of this sort of manipulation and only your imagination will limit the number of games you can play and get away with.

Use a small spoon to handle the eggs you plan to switch. Children's play sets often provide finch-egg-sized spoons. You should experience no trouble by adding one or two eggs from another nest to a clutch of societies which was started about the same time. A few days more or less for an unincubated egg will not materially effect its chances, but the closer in time, the better.

Mark moved eggs with a date or a number. Keep records, eventually the sterile males and the producers of thin-shelled eggs will be found and culled out or helped.

If you work with several species or more than a few pairs of birds, you might want to use several colors to aid in keeping track. Felt or fiber tip pens are inexpensive and safe to use. Simply mark a small number or a date in a particular color on each egg you switch, and then record this information in a permanent record book or card file. Most finch eggs you will encounter are the same color—a pale creamy pinkish white, and although the size does vary with species, it also varies with the age of the hen, so you cannot rely on egg size observations to determine what you transferred where.

Before you advance very far in proficiency as a breeder of societies you will be asked or you will wonder why you don't bring up waifs or why you don't use an incubator and avoid the problems of non-broody birds and deserted nests.

To begin with, society finches don't usually neglect either eggs or young. If they do, the fault is usually something within your control. Check for noises, odors, distracting lights, vermin, diseases, disturbances by other animals and then correct the problem at the source. This, in the long run, will be much easier than any scheme for substituting a machine for a pair of parent birds.

Secondly, your effort input will be disproportionately high when you compare it with your success ratio. The best parents for society finches are society finches. Remember also that these birds have been domesticated for centuries. You are doing something which is interesting and challenging but not at all new. If your birds are not producing, it is probably not their fault but rather your neglect of some simple little detail.

The third aspect of the answer to the hypothetical question about artificial rearing is that it is tremendously difficult. For one thing, a day-old chick is no larger than its egg—a matter of only a few grams—hardly larger than a green pea. You would have to be a micromanipulator to get food into its mouth. Then there is the problem of food and the bacteria which are not present in the egg but must establish themselves in the digestive tract to convert the grain into energy and protoplasm. No easy task.

Survival of the most fit is also a factor in the problem of the waif. It is possible that the rejected chick was rejected because of a deformity which the parents recognized.

Predatory birds and large parrots have been raised by dedicated humans, but here size and diet make the difference. Remember also that society finches are not precocious. They are hatched blind and naked, as contrasted to waterfowl and poultry whose chicks can walk and feed themselves soon after they emerge from their shells.

(1) Two chicks are sleeping; the third has raised its head, but its eyes have not yet fully opened. Here (2) an unrelated adult society finch is feeding the chicks.

These chicks (3) will be fed every forty minutes. They will start crying for more food thirty minutes after each meal. A foster parent (4) about to feed three squeakers. Note the ear opening on the chick nearest the bottom of the picture.

3

4

American Avicultural Societies

Much of your fun and satisfaction and help will come from membership in an avicultural society. If you want to breed society finches, you should budget some time for joining a club *and* attending meetings *and* participating in the shows. Remember that no one is an island, and furthermore, many of your seemingly insurmountable problems have probably been solved many times before.

Also, subscribe to a magazine if your society does not publish one of its own. To make a beginning you should start with a sample copy of the *American Cage Bird Magazine,* which publishes a list of clubs in every issue. Write to the club or association secretary whose address or name most closely matches your interest.

In the United States the three leading avicultural magazines are *American Cage Bird Magazine* (3449 N. Western Ave., Chicago, Illinois 60618); *The A.F.A. Watchbird* (published by the American Federation of Aviculture Inc., P.O. Box 1125, Garden Grove, California 92642); and *Bird World* (11552 Hartsook St., North Hollywood, California 91601).

In Great Britain the leading magazine is *Cage and Aviary Birds* (Surrey House, 1 Throwley Way, St. Sutton, Surrey, England).

Inexpensive and usually in good supply, society finches are considered by many to be excellent birds for preparing beginners in the finch fancy to gain enough experience to deal with more expensive finch species such as this broad-tailed paradise whydah, *Steganura orientalis.*

1   2

The hen bird flying (1) in to feed the squeakers. Note the dark crescent-shaped mark on the upper palate. Each species of these small seed-eating finches has a distinctive palate marking. The points on the tail feathers (2) are the source of the specific scientific name *acuticauda* (*acuti* = sharpened, pointed; *cauda* = tail) applied to the society finch. One dark bird fell out of the nest (3) and was killed when it hit the floor four feet below. The dark bird (4) will very soon leave the nest.

3

4

RECOMMENDED READING

BUILDING AN AVIARY, (TFH/PS-763), Prof. Carl Naether and Dr. Matthew M. Vriends, ISBN 0-87666-963-1. This excellent how-to-book offers practical suggestions and step-by-step instructions for equipping and constructing an aviary to suit the needs and tastes of the individual fancier. Written for all birdkeepers, beginners and veterans alike. Gives excellent information about which species are compatible. Hard cover, 5½ x 8, 160 pages; 50 color photos, 38 b/w photos.

BIRD DISEASES: An Introduction to the Study of Birds in Health and Disease, (TFH/H-964), Drs. L. Arnall and I.F. Keymer, ISBN 0-87666-950-X. A highly specialized book which requires a thorough education in biology to be understood, but experienced bird lovers can recognize symptoms and diseases from the many illustrations. Hard cover, 6 x 9, 528 pages; 99 color photos, 304 b/w photos.

DISEASES OF BIRDS, (TFH/AP-926), Robert Stroud, ISBN 0-87666-435-4. There is no other book which can help the layman more in the diagnosis, control and treatment of bird diseases than this classic reference volume by the Birdman of Alcatraz. Hard cover, 8½ x 5½, 483 pages; 87 line illustrations.

BUDGERIGARS, (TFH/KW-011), Georg A. Radtke, ISBN 0-87666-984-4. A considerable amount of new material, including but not limited to additional photographs, has been added to the literal German-English translation of this very thorough book by an author with forty years experience with parakeets. Hard cover, 5½ x 8, 96 pages; 43 color photos, many b/w photos.

BUDGERIGAR HANDBOOK, (TFH/H-901), Ernest H. Hart, ISBN 0-87666-414-1. Almost every color variety is shown in full color photographs; breeding, showing, and every other subject of importance for the budgie enthusiast is completely covered. 5½ x 8½, 251 pages; 104 color photos, 67 b/w photos.

AUSTRALIAN SHELL PARAKEETS, (TFH/KW-036), Earl Schneider and Dr. Matthew M. Vriends, ISBN 0-87666-998-4. Covers every important aspect of maintenance, feeding, housing, breeding, and disease control.

CANARY VARIETIES, (TFH/KW-024), Klaus Speicher, ISBN 0-87666-993-3. Originally published in German, this very thorough book treats canary varieties rarely mentioned in other texts. Most species are shown in full color photographs. Hard cover, 5½ x 8, 96 pages; heavily illustrated in both color and black and white.

ALL ABOUT CANARIES, (TFH/PS-315), Irene Evans, ISBN 0-87666-953-4. For the beginning canary owner, this book covers metabolism, preening, housing, feeding, handling, and teaching tricks. Soft cover, 5½ x 8, 96 pages; 32 color photos, 41 b/w photos.

ENCYCLOPEDIA OF CANARIES, (TFH/H-967), G.T. Dodwell, ISBN 0-87666-952-6. This book is intended for the new canary fancier. It covers breeding systems, heredity and environment, types of exhibition, birdrooms, and cage fitting. Hard cover, 5½ x 8, 281 pages; 48 color photos, 28 b/w photos.

DISEASES OF CANARIES, (TFH/PS-640), Robert Stroud [The Birdman of Alcatraz], ISBN 0-87666-436-2. This book discusses everything of interest to canary keepers who want to maintain their birds' good health, from a complete discussion of good feeding programs and canaries' anatomy through detailed treatments of every canary injury and disease. Hard cover, 5½ x 8, 239 pages.

ALL ABOUT FINCHES AND RELATED SEED-EATING BIRDS, (TFH/PS-765), Ian Harman and Dr. Matthew M. Vriends, ISBN 0-87666-965-8. A good introductory book on the care and breeding of finches, with more than 100 birds fully identified. Breeding requirements are also treated. Hard cover, 5½ x 8, 224 pages; 53 color photos, 65 b/w photos, 16 line drawings.

INTRODUCTION TO FINCHES AND SOFTBILLS, (TFH/PS-648), Hank Bates and Bob Busenbark, ISBN 0-87666-423-0. For those just starting out with finches as a hobby, this will guide them through the better selection of various finches and will instruct the reader in the proper care and diet to avoid many errors which are commonly made. Soft cover, 8 x 5½, 96 pages; 32 color photos, 12 b/w photos.

FINCHES AND SOFT-BILLED BIRDS, (TFH/H-908), Henry Bates and Robert Busenbark, ISBN 0-87666-421-4. Every important soft-billed cage bird is discussed and illustrated in color. Used throughout the world as an identification guide. Hard cover, 5½ x 8½, 735 pages; 246 color photos, 159 b/w photos.

AUSTRALIAN FINCHES, (TFH/KW-027), Curt af Enehjelm, ISBN 0-87666-987-9. Covers the keeping, breeding, and managing of these species as well as their chacteristics and behavior. Hard cover, 5½ x 8, 96 pages; heavily illustrated in both color and black and white.

GUIDE TO MYNAHS, (TFH/PS-633), Hank Bates and Bob Busenbark, ISBN 0-87666-425-7. A very fine guidebook for owners and potential owners of mynahs with chapters on diet, care, feeding, training, breeding, diseases and cures. Soft cover, 8 x 5½, 96 pages; 56 b/w photos, 9 line illustrations.

PARROTS AND RELATED BIRDS, (TFH/H-912), Henry J. Bates and Robert L. Busenbark, Third Edition edited and expanded by Dr. Matthew M. Vriends, ISBN 0-87666-967-4. This book has more color photographs of parrots than any other book. New editions are issued regularly, with new color photos added to each new edition. This third edition includes updated nomenclature, and has been restructured for easier reading. Hard cover, 5½ x 8½, 494 pages; 160 color photos, 107 b/w photos.

PARROTS OF THE WORLD, (TFH/PS-753), Joseph M. Forshaw, ISBN 0-87666-959-3. This immense book covers every species and subspecies of parrot in the world, including those recently extinct. Almost 500 species and subspecies are illustrated in full color on large color plates. Hard cover, 9½ x 12½, 584 pages; almost 300 large color plates, many line illustrations.

PHEASANT BREEDING AND CARE, (TFH/AP-6450), Jean Dalacour, ISBN 0-87666-434-6. A most useful, descriptive and authoritative volume that even the most advanced fancier should have close at hand. The book is accompanied by a large separate color chart showing 45 species in full color. New edition. Hard cover, 5½ x 8, 192 pages; 72 color photos, 37 b/w photos.

WILD PIGEONS AND DOVES, (TFH/AP-6810), Dr. Jean Delacour, ISBN 0-87666-968-2. Covers all types of pigeons and doves from the standpoints of their maintenance and husbandry in captivity as well as their fascinating habits in the wild. Soft cover, 5½ x 8, 160 pages; heavily illustrated in both color and black and white.